IMAGES
of America

SAN FRANCISCO'S
BAYVIEW
HUNTERS POINT

Tricia O'Brien

ARCADIA
PUBLISHING

Copyright © 2005 by Tricia O'Brien
ISBN 978-1-5316-1628-1

Published by Arcadia Publishing
Charleston, South Carolina

Library of Congress Catalog Card Number: 2005926986

For all general information contact Arcadia Publishing at:
Telephone 843-853-2070
Fax 843-853-0044
E-mail sales@arcadiapublishing.com
For customer service and orders:
Toll-Free 1-888-313-2665

Visit us on the Internet at www.arcadiapublishing.com

IMAGES
of America

SAN FRANCISCO'S BAYVIEW HUNTERS POINT

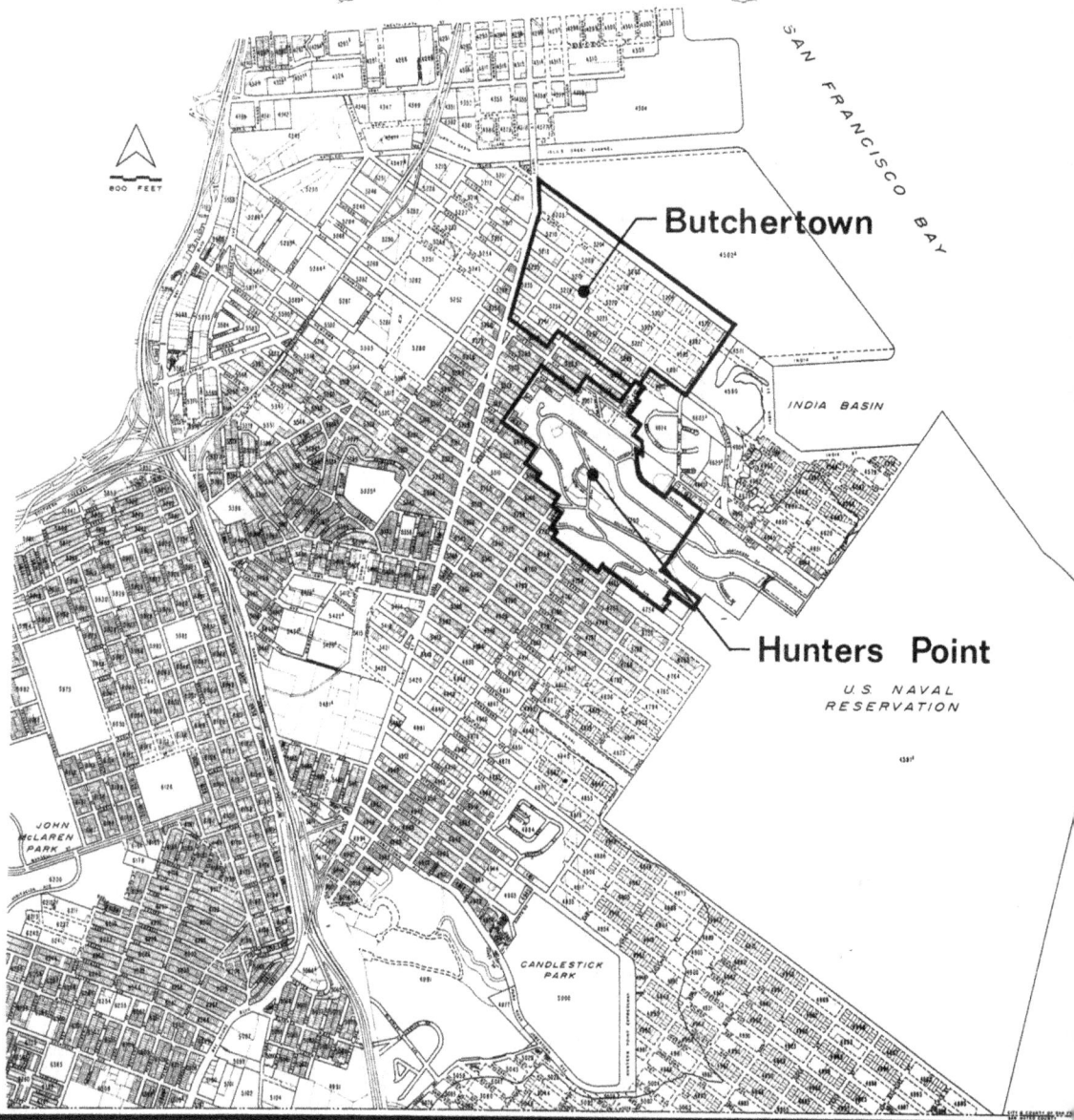

BOUNDARY MAP

This is an April 1967 boundary map of the Bayview Hunters Point area. (Courtesy of the San Francisco Redevelopment Agency.)

CONTENTS

ACKNOWLEDGMENTS

I would like to express my appreciation and thanks to those who shared their photographs, memories, and time to make this book possible: John Allemand, Rene "Flip" Allemand, William Armanino, Al Baglietto, Gary Banks, Linda Blacketer, Linda Brooks Burton, Barbara Diamond Camp, Adrian Card, Lou Castelli, Sam Catania, Cab Covey, Wendy Cox, Fr. Patrick Coyle, Dan Dodt, Rita Dunn, Edie Epps, Angela Tanforan Fabbri, Erin Farrell, Lillian and Steve Flahavan, Greg Gaar, Rico Ghilardi, Gloria Grover Sr., Grace Grima, Bernie Hagan, Margaret "Slim" Hannah, Muriel Andrade Hebert, Vic Herbert, Eric Higgs, Oscar James, Betty Jones, Allen Jordan, Walter Kreutzer, Ed and Edie Laboure, Jon Legallet, Jok Legallet, Lisa Larkins, Antoinette Longa, Larry Ludwigsen, Mary Mauer, Gene and Gloria Maffei, Edward Mazzei, Raymond McGrath, Irene Molinari, Louise Molinari, Norma Nessier, Beverly Nielsen, Peggy Andrade O'Brien, Tim and Rita O'Brien, Peg O'Connell, Rita Oosterman, Yvonne Picard, Mary Ratcliff, Sally Ross, Lita Jane Tynan Smith, Lorraine Scullion, Jack Tillmany, John Tinker, Paul Trimble, Joyce Turner, Robert Turner, Lorri Ungaretti, Joe Ursino, Giacomo James Ursino, Dolores Williams. Also, to Siobhan Boyle, who helped scan, research, call people, and performed all the other tasks I asked her to do as my intern for her January winter break term. Thank you mom, dad, and Margaret. And a very special thanks to my Simon and Sebastian.

The Bayview Hunters Point neighborhood was home to several generations of my family. The area is full of rich and varied history. Everyone I interviewed told me it was a great place to grow up. Many have fond memories of life in this part of San Francisco.

INTRODUCTION

San Francisco's Bayview Hunters Point takes a look at the early days of the area, including Butchertown; the shipbuilding before, during, and after World War II; the people, churches, schools, and businesses that shaped the neighborhood; and offers a glance at what the neighborhood is like today.

Bayview Hunters Point encompasses the southeast corner of San Francisco. From the north, the area starts at Islais Creek or First Bridge (although some will argue it starts at Cesar Chavez) and runs to the San Francisco–San Mateo county line.

In 1775, Juan Bautista de Ayala, captain of the *San Carlos*, was commissioned by Spain to make a survey of the San Francisco Bay. As part of this survey, Ayala asked his second mate, Juan Bautista Aguirre, to investigate the southern portion of the bay including the area he named La Punta Concha (Seashell Point), now known as Hunters Point. Years later, Spanish settlers renamed the area La Punta Avisadera (The Beacon Point). Ohlone Indians lived on the hill then.

During Spanish and Mexican ownership, the Bayview Hunters Point area was inhabited mainly by grazing livestock owned by Mission Dolores. Most of the area was part of a land grant consisting of 4,446 acres called Rincon de las Salinas y Potrero Viejo (Place of the Salt Works and Old Pasture), which the Mexican government awarded in 1839 to Jose Cornelio de Bernal.

Early land developers Dr. John Townsend and Corneille de Boom, who envisioned developments in "South San Francisco" before it was known as Hunter's Point, convinced Bernal to become a real estate developer and sell his land grants. In 1849, Robert Eugene Hunter and his brother Phillip Schuyler Hunter arrived from New York and became agents for Bernal. John, a third brother, arrived later. Bernal's residential effort failed, but the Hunter brothers stayed in the area in their house and dairy farm near Griffith Street and Oakdale Avenue. While it is generally accepted that the area is named for the Hunter brothers, some argue the area is named Hunters Point because of the actual hunters who hunted on the hill.

After the 1906 earthquake and fire, many who were burned out of their homes ventured to this part of town because of the availability of land. It was unofficially known as South San Francisco until 1909, when it started to make itself known as Bayview. The town formerly known as Baden incorporated itself—officially claiming the name South San Francisco. At the same time, the 1909 street-naming commission was in the process of changing street names in the Bayview, Mission, and Sunset districts to eliminate the confusion that three sets of numbered and three sets of alphabetical street names was causing. Irving and Judah were originally proposed for the Bayview district, but ended up in the Sunset. The commission boldly named two streets for men who were still alive—Bancroft Street, named for California historian Hubert Howe Bancroft, and Keith Street, named for the popular California artist.

When San Francisco was awarded the honor of hosting the 1915 Panama-Pacific International Exposition, the Bayview Hunters Point area was suggested as a location to hold the event. The Marina district won the bid instead.

Butchertown came to the Bayview Hunters Point district in the mid-1850s, when the city started moving the slaughterhouses south, away from the heart of San Francisco. Butchertown was a big employer for the neighborhood. Slaughterhouses, tanneries, tallow works, and butchers dominated the area. The meat from steers, sheep, and hogs was sold all over California and Japan.

Cowboys rode their horses through the streets and drove cattle from the first bridge over Islais Creek when they came off the barges, to the corrals on Silver Avenue, or from the railroad stop on the west side of Third Street (once known as Railroad Avenue) to the corrals on the east side of Third Street. Every day they drove the animals down to the slaughterhouses. They also drove them up Hunters Point Hill to graze. At one time, there were 3,500 people working in the slaughterhouses. Evans Avenue and Third Street was the heart of Butchertown. There was the H. Moffat Company on Third Street and Arthur Avenue, then down the street at Third Street and Evans was the William Taaffe and Company. Charlie "Monkey Charlie" Rosenburg owned a small slaughterhouse as well. Across the street was Allan and Pyle, which eventually became James Allan & Sons. There was also Roth and Blum, who then sold the business to the Alpert Packing Company before it went to James Allan. Eventually, Levitt and Hyde took over Monkey Charlie's. Al Levitan had an office on Third Street and Evans where he would salt the hides and send them to Japan. Next to him were San Francisco Casing and Peale Casing. Across the street was Zenith Meant, which Safeway took over before selling to James Allan. On Third Street and Hudson Streets were O'Dea Feed, Grain, and Fuel and Denike's Tavern, a well-known restaurant and bar. On the next corner was Dr. Nellie Null. She brought a majority of the Butchertown population into the world and continued to care for them throughout their lives. Today, the India Basin Industrial Park sits where the heart of Butchertown once lived.

The shipyard portion of what is now Hunters Point Naval Shipyard began as two simple dry docks. Chinese shrimp boats lined the shore. Along the waterfront, as well as at the dry docks, individuals built their own boatbuilding and repair companies. Soon after, corporations arrived, then the U.S. Navy took over the dry docks and gated a large portion of the Hunters Point area, significantly changing the entire dynamic of not only the docks, but the entire district.

From 1860 to 1910, scow schooners were big business. They were the most effective and efficient way to move hay, lumber, bricks, produce, and other essential items needed throughout the Bay Area. Names such as "Pop" Anderson, Johnson J. Dirks, Erickson, O. F. L. Farenkamp, Ervin, Goebel, William Munder, Siemer, Thomsen, August and Willie Schultze, William Stone, Nichols, and Weaver had their shipyards, Islais Creek and Hunters Point, to build and repair the scow schooners. Fred Siemer's *Alma* is probably the most famous schooner to come out of Hunters Point. It was named for one of his daughters. In 1988, *Alma* was designated a national historic landmark, and it is now at the Hyde Street Pier as part of the San Francisco Maritime National Historic Park's fleet.

Both world wars contributed to the growth of shipbuilding at Hunters Point as San Francisco focused on servicing much larger ships, especially navy ones. During World War II, a new ship was built every 24 hours. There were also six docks for submarines. Most of the smaller boatbuilders contributed to the war effort.

Three churches dominated the neighborhood: All Hallows for the Irish, St. Paul the Shipwreck for the Maltese, and Joan of Arc for the French. The churches played a major role in community life, and each church had a school associated with it.

The people are what really made the Bayview Hunters Point district so unique. They were a league of nations who came from places like Ireland, Italy, France, Malta, Greece, Mexico, and Germany. Some spoke English and some did not, but somehow people communicated. Nicknames were common, almost required. Everyone knew each other at least by sight, and everyone looked out for each other. It was a great place to live. In the summer, it could take two hours to go two blocks. Many people sat in front of their garages to visit. The smell of homemade wine lingered in the air. Kids played ball in the park. A Sunday family outing usually included buying a pound of shrimp wrapped in newspaper for a quarter. The only thing to beware of in that part of town was the shift in the wind that could blow a nasty stench from the tallow works.

One of the most famous Butchertown boys is baseball player and manager Frank "Lefty" O'Doul. Dr. Nellie Null delivered most of the babies and tended to them into adulthood. She often "forgot" to bill clients less fortunate. Mr. Sharman, or "One-Nail Sharman," built many homes in Bayview. His belief was to never put two nails when you could get by with only one. His houses are still around today. Mr. Graziani hollered the phrase "rags, bottles, sacks" to collect what would now be known as recycling. The milkman and the iceman delivered daily. On hot days, kids would climb in the iceman's truck to eat ice shavings. He had great big tongs and a leather strap across his back. Once a month, a little Italian man came around selling potatoes, sometimes for 35¢ a sack and sometimes for 50¢, depending on the season.

Third Street, formerly Railroad Avenue, served as the main street for the Bayview district. Most anything one needed could be found here. The Butchertown portion of Third Street stretched from Arthur Avenue to Kirkwood Avenue. The shopping portion was mainly from La Salle Avenue to Williams Avenue. Throughout the years business came and went, but not too frequently. For a while, cowboys on horses were common on Third Street.

The Dutch Mill was the place to go for a big scoop of homemade ice cream and to hang out with friends.

Bayview Hunters Point has gone through tremendous change over the years. Today residential, commercial, and industrial areas still comprise the neighborhood. It boasts the largest percentage of homeowners in San Francisco, the best weather in the city, and high growth potential. It also has the largest concentration of public housing and environmental issues, and some of the city's poorest residents. Unlike the past, only 25 percent of the residents work within the neighborhood.

There are no dominant churches as there were in the past, but there are many churches that provide a strong spiritual and community-focused influence. The churches no longer have schools beside them, but the city has committed to improving the public schools in the district. Called "dream schools," the focus is on more structure and higher academic standards.

The neighborhood is home to four San Francisco landmarks: the Bayview Opera House, designated December 8, 1968; Hunters Point Springs/Albion Brewery, designated April 5, 1974; the Sylvester House, designated April 5, 1974; and the Quinn House, designated July 6, 1974.

Since the late 1960s, redevelopment efforts have been presented for such projects as enhancing the temporary housing units built during World War II, luring private and community investments to the neighborhood by offering affordable real estate, and increasing access to the area through new highways and expanded roads. Some efforts have been successful. In the 1980s, the urban-renewal agency built nearly 1,500 subsidized homes. Today, the Third Street Light Rail project is in process, and churches and other nonprofit organizations are working diligently to provide programs to assist families with economic assistance, job placement, community relations, and other family needs.

This section of the bay used to be a thriving waterfront, a gateway to Butchertown, the home of the shrimp-processing industry, and an active boat-building and repair area. A variety of vessels, including shrimp boats, schooners, houseboats, and ferries, could be found in this section of the Bay on a regular basis. The Hunters Point dry docks are in the distance. (Courtesy of Rene "Flip" Allemand.)

One

THE EARLY YEARS

Prior to 1868, not much more than this serpentine rock and the Ohlone Indians populated Hunters Point. Shipyards and slaughterhouses started to make their way to the area in the mid- to late-1800s. Soon houses and livestock started to populate Hunters Point Hill. The 1906 earthquake started the next wave of new occupants to this part of the city. (Courtesy of a private collector.)

In the late 1880s, the Bayview Hotel was the place to go. San Franciscans rode the Bayview–Potrero Railroad from the Montgomery and Post station to the Bayview racetrack developed by Leland Stanford and Charles Crocker in 1888, near what is now Third Street and Williams Avenue. The hotel was next to the racetrack. (Courtesy of a private collector.)

In 1886, All Hallows Church was established, and Rev. Timothy Fitzpatrick was the first pastor. Originally the Catholics had to travel to St. Patrick's on Mission Street for mass. (Courtesy of All Hallows Church.)

The Daughters of Charity of St. Vincent De Paul ran Mount St. Joseph and Mount St. Joseph Infant Asylum. In 1873, they sold the Market and Montgomery Streets property and moved nearly 300 orphans to this building in the Silver Terrace area. Now both sections could be under one roof. While it was known as Mount St. Joseph, the legal name was the Roman Catholic Orphan Asylum. They survived the 1906 earthquake and fire with no damage; however, a 1910 fire destroyed the building. Everyone escaped except one little girl who ran back to retrieve her beloved doll. The orphans lived in temporary housing until the fall of 1912 when their new building was completed in the same location. (Courtesy of a private collector.)

In the early days, people called the Bayview Hunters Point area South San Francisco. The South San Francisco Opera House was built by the Masons as part of their Masonic Temple and was originally intended as an amusement center. It is the city's first opera house, although no operas were ever actually performed in this building. It was more of a meeting place for groups such as the Native Sons and Native Daughters. However, some performers did take the stage to entertain the locals, including David Belasco who went on to become well-known in New York. Pawnee Bill's Medicine Show and several old minstrels also appeared on this stage. Mrs. Collins ran a dry goods store in the front section. (Courtesy of Jack Tillmany.)

In 1896, the South San Francisco Brewery was located on the northwest corner of Railroad Avenue and Fourteenth Avenue South. The famous South San Francisco Lager Beer was made here, but Prohibition forced many breweries like this one to close. (Courtesy of Dr. Larry Ludwigsen.)

In 1900, the John Acher Saloon at Third and Revere Streets was a popular place to get a large glass of South San Francisco Lager Beer. This location was home to several bars, but in the early 1940s a bank moved in. (Courtesy of Dr. Larry Ludwigsen.)

Processions along Third Street were common. This c. 1900 photograph shows a May Day celebration. (Courtesy of Dr. Larry Ludwigsen.)

This 1908 photograph looks west from Railroad Avenue (Third Street) and Quesada Avenue as a parade marches by. The steeple of All Hallows Church can be seen in the background. (Courtesy of Dr. Larry Ludwigsen.)

This view is looking north from Railroad Avenue (Third Street) and Quesada Avenue. The horse corral on the right eventually became the site of the Bay View Federal Savings and Loan. (Courtesy of Dr. Larry Ludwigsen.)

Built in 1861, the Oakdale Bar, which eventually became the Old Clam House on Bayshore Boulevard, is still known as the oldest restaurant in its original location in San Francisco. Originally it was closer to the waterline and to a creek, but landfill has increased its distance from the bay. (Courtesy of a private collector.)

Anna Imhof Zwyssig and her husband, Ambrose Zurfluh, owned the Old Clam House. Every morning, Anna prepared a luncheon buffet of homemade soup, hard-boiled eggs, French rolls, and a variety of lunch meats for the customers. For 5¢, the customers would receive a large beer and as much of the buffet as they wanted. Anna passed away on June 13, 1913. (Courtesy of Beverly Nielsen.)

The Old Clam House was built in a muddy, swampy area, so Ambrose Zurfluh built a pair of stilts for his sons to use to cross the street. When the 1906 earthquake hit, the Old Clam House luckily experienced little damage—except for the now famous crooked floor from the floor boards rising up and coming back down. An Army officer approached Ambrose and told him that some homeless people from downtown would be staying in his cellar, which was a regular practice after the earthquake with the amount of people who were displaced. He and his wife welcomed them, some for over a year. (Courtesy of Beverly Nielsen.)

A decent road had to be paved to reach the dry docks along Innes Avenue. The Albion Ale and Porter Brewery (tall building at right), founded by John Hamlyn Burnell, was along Innes Avenue near Griffith Street. Spring water pulled from under Hunters Point Hill was stored in caverns alongside the brewery. Master brewer Burnell won several awards for his ale and porter at the 1915 Pan-Pacific International Exposition. With Prohibition, the brewery closed and later the building crumbled. In 1940, French sculptor Adrien Voison bought the brewery and restored it to its original look. (Courtesy of a private collector.)

This is a September 1917 image of the Hunters Point School, located on Innes Avenue. It was a two-room grammar school for local students. After Prohibition, children used to sneak into the abandoned caverns on the side of the Albion Brewery next door. (Courtesy of a private collector.)

In 1933, men are leveling the hill near Gilman Avenue to make way for new developments in the area. (Courtesy of a private collector.)

In 1865, Elizabeth O'Brien became an early resident of Bayview. By 1876, she had a house built on Galvez Street. Elizabeth lived upstairs and a Mrs. Griffith lived downstairs. (Courtesy of Robert and Joyce Turner.)

This is the view of Quesada Avenue looking west from Third Street in June 1919. (Courtesy of a private collector.)

In 1920, there was only a smattering of houses on the Bayview Hill near Key Avenue. (Courtesy of a private collector.)

This is a January 1924 view looking north from Meade and Keith Streets to the Bayview Hill. (Courtesy of a private collector.)

A few more houses expanded the settlement on the hill. (Courtesy of a private collector.)

One could view ships in the bay at Galvez Avenue and Coleman Street, as seen in this June 1942 photograph. (Courtesy of a private collector.)

During World War II, sailors were a common sight at the end of Hunters Point Boulevard at Galvez Avenue and Coleman Street. (Courtesy of a private collector.)

Housing and lot prices in 1942 were a little different from what they are today. This lot on Galvez Avenue and Coleman Street was selling for $5 down or $175 for the full lot. (Courtesy of a private collector.)

India Basin was home to boats, boatyards, and slaughterhouses. Ferries shuttling people to places like Vallejo and Alameda left from this location as well as boats carrying building supplies, hay, produce, and the necessities to the Bay Area. Eventually it would become the dumping grounds for such vessels when they became obsolete. This photograph also shows much more water in the area than is found today due to land fill. (Courtesy of a private collector.)

Two

BUTCHERTOWN

In 1936, cowboys herd sheep up Innes Avenue to graze on Hunters Point Hill as seven-year-old Dick Lawless looks on from his front yard. The slaughterhouses didn't have to worry about feeding the animals because there was so much grass on the hills for them to eat. (Courtesy of Mary Lou Lawless Mauer.)

James Allan and Sons Meat Packing Company used this truck and others like it to deliver meat to various butcher shops around town. (Courtesy of Margaret "Slim" Hannah.)

Ken Myles, Robert Turner, and Frank Budessa show off the sides of beef at James Allan and Sons. Robert Turner started working at this slaughterhouse in 1931 at age 17 and stayed until 1976. (Courtesy of Joyce and Robert Turner.)

James Allan and Sons Meat Packing Company at Newhall and Evans Streets was one of the largest slaughterhouses in the area. (Courtesy of San Francisco History Center, San Francisco Public Library; photographer Al Canterbury.)

On the killing floor of the slaughterhouse, from left to right, are John Mendez, Billy Marchi, Steve Barney, Ed Laboure, Murphy Johnny Straub, Johnny Mike Marchi (the boss), and Dutch Carl (a hide dropper). Standing under the lamb racks in back is the salesman, Frenchi. Notice the gut truck next to the steer for the heart, liver, and lungs. (Courtesy of Ed Laboure.)

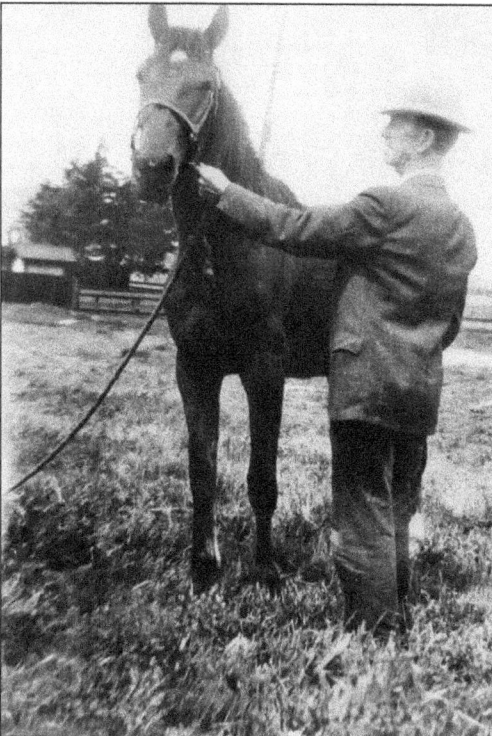

Cows are being herded into the slaughterhouse in this 1929 image. Cattle often came off the trains a couple of blocks away from the slaughterhouses and cowboys would herd them to busy Third Street. Every so often one would escape and cause havoc with traffic and kids trying to get to school—not that the kids minded. (Courtesy of the San Francisco History Center, San Francisco Public Library.)

Ed "Knockers" Sullivan was a corral man at H. Moffat Company. On Sundays, he would dress up in a clean pair of Levis, a blue shirt with his Bull Durham sack in the pocket, and a 10-gallon hat. He would stand in front of the bar on Third Street talking to people all day. Every hour he would go into the bar for a double shot. That was his Sunday. Monday mornings he would be back in the slaughterhouse "knocking beef." (Courtesy of Margaret "Slim" Hannah.)

The building in the center of this photograph at 1490 Fairfax Avenue once housed Roth and Blum, one of the original slaughterhouses in the area. It was then sold to Alpert Packing Company, who later sold to James Allan, making it the largest sheep and hog slaughterhouse in the area. (Courtesy of a private collector.)

Steve Flahavan worked at the H. Moffat Company but kept a horse behind James Allan and Sons located at Third Street and Evans. Flahavan built the barn with the help of his friend Vin Mahoney. (Courtesy of Steve Flahavan.)

Dominique Legallet opened Legallet Wool Pullery and Tannery in Butchertown in 1879 on Sixth Avenue (Kirkwood) and Quint Street, and in 1930 moved to this location at 1099 Quesada Avenue. Dominique started the business while still living in France, but moved to San Francisco for a better life. While watching the men at the slaughterhouses throw hides away, he knew there was a great opportunity to restart his business and brought men from France to work in his tannery. (Courtesy of Jon and Jok Legallet.)

Dominique sent for his three nephews, Eugene, George and Arthur, to help him run the operation. During World War II, the Navy took control of the water outside of the tannery and filled it in, increasing the distance of the tannery to the bay. (Courtesy of Jon and Jok Legallet.)

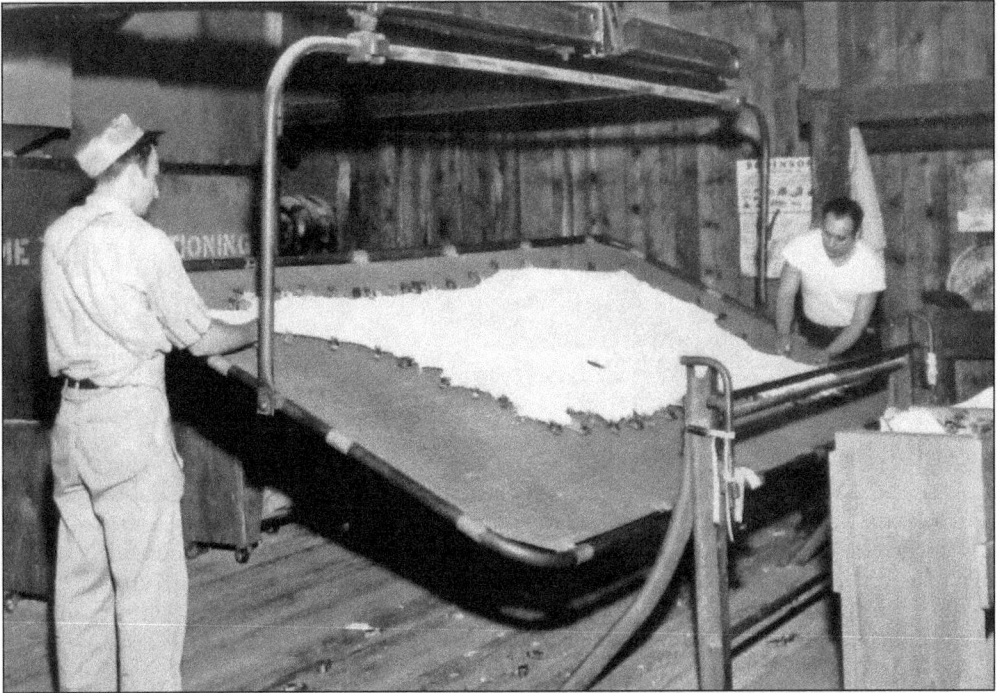

At the Legallet wool house, workers would bring hides in, stretch them out, and paint them with a green solution. This solution would burn a hole through a person's pants if dropped, so it couldn't be touched; it was best just to let it dry then shake it off. The next day, the hides were placed on racks and the wool was removed. The remaining hide was then thrown in a vat and washed. (Courtesy of Jon and Jok Legallet.)

After the hides were free of hair and washed, they were hung to dry for a day. (Courtesy of Jon and Jok Legallet.)

Cyril Denike (left center with light hat, to the right of the man with the gun, hat, and plaid shirt) and his Butchertown "bad men" pretend to raid a local bank and make off with thousands of dollars in gold nuggets. Holding the nugget sack is Fred Nickelson. Directly in front with arms reaching to the sky is Atello Armanino. This was part of a poster promoting the 1939 Bayview Stampede from February 14 to 17 to celebrate the World's Fair. (Courtesy of Dr. Larry Ludwigsen.)

The Butchertown Boys take a day off from their hard work to celebrate the Bayview Stampede for the World's Fair. (Courtesy of Dr. Larry Ludwigsen.)

Miller and Lux was one of the first companies in Butchertown. Started by Henry Miller and Charles Lux, their agricultural corporation covered a large portion of California, but the headquarters were in San Francisco. Their meatpacking operation in Butchertown was the largest west of Chicago. In 1900, they were the only agricultural company to be ranked among the top 200 largest industrial companies in the nation. (Courtesy of Rita Oosterman.)

To celebrate the World's Fair in San Francisco, workers at Legallet Tannery created a float and dressed as 49ers for the parade. Legallet is the dapper man in the suit in the back row. (Courtesy of Jon and Jok Legallet.)

The rodeo, held next door to the Legallet Tannery, was a popular place to show off skills or to just hang out. (Courtesy of Rita Dunn.)

Harry Dunn, Raymond "Lovey" Dunn, and Ducky Hughes (on his horse) enjoy a day at the corral. (Courtesy of Rita Dunn.)

Nellie Tanforan was an amazing horsewoman. This 1934 photograph was taken at Tortilla Flats on Hudson Avenue when she was 20 years old. When she wasn't working, she could be found at the corrals riding her horse or racing at the Polo Fields in Golden Gate Park. She worked for Moffat's Meat Packing Company, and during the war was a welder at the shipyard. (Courtesy of Nellie Tanforan Fabbri.)

Nellie Tanforan and Margaret Ford are racing to the finish line. Nellie took first place, as she usually did, in this race. (Courtesy of Nellie Tanforan Fabbri.)

This group of friends enjoying a day out at the roping corral in 1945, from left to right, are (first row) Jim Quinones, Harry Dunn, singer Guy "Arkie" Mitchell, Dan Carey, Pete Quinones, and Bob Mason; (second row) Barney Hensel, Winnie Dunn's father, and Winnie. (Courtesy of Margaret "Slim" Hannah.)

John Olsen, of Olsen Nolte Saddle Shop, was often found at the corral. Originally the shop was called Nolte Olsen Saddle Shop, but when Al Nolte passed away in 1939, John switched the names to Olsen Nolte. (Courtesy Margaret "Slim" Hannah.)

Olsen Nolte Saddle Shop was founded in 1937 by Al Nolte. He was later joined by John E. Olsen. When Al Nolte passed away, Walt Goldsmith took over production. The company continued to support the neighborhood's needs until 1958 when it moved to San Carlos where it still conducts business. (Courtesy of the Olsen Nolte Archives.)

Here's a peek inside the saddle shop. It was a convenient retail outlet for cowboys because of its close proximity to the slaughterhouses. It was originally located four to five blocks down from the Opera House, but in 1938 it actually moved into the Opera House. The retail shop was downstairs and manufacturing was upstairs. Olsen Nolte was one of 10 prominent saddle companies that made fine silver parade saddles.

Ducky Hughes Jr. followed in his father's footsteps as a special cop in Bayview. Some of the first lawmen were Big Dick and his counterpart "Shorty," followed by Ducky Hughes Sr., and then Ducky Hughes Jr. They kept the streets safe and rattled all the doors to make sure there was no trouble. (Courtesy of Margaret "Slim" Hannah.)

Leo's Hotel and Restaurant, or "Papa Leo's" as it was more commonly known, was run by an eccentric Frenchman. Every day at 11:30 a.m., he would close and lock the doors. If patrons weren't inside on time they didn't get served his famous lunch that he cooked himself. In the 1940s, he served salad, pasta, an entree, a tenth of wine, French bread, and a piece of cheese for $1.25. The bar served only beer, wine, and vermouth. Seen here on horseback are Sal, Glen Parker, Pete Ritchie (who played for the Seals), Barney Hensel, Coke Vanucchi, and Margaret (Mag) Chigem. (Courtesy of Margaret "Slim" Hannah.)

Three

SHIPYARDS

This photograph was taken around 1866 at Hunters Point in what is believed to be William Munder's boatyard. There are three schooners here, one in the water, one being repaired in the yard, and another being built. Picnicking on the hill was a popular pastime. Houses and people were scarce, and the waterline was still untouched. (Courtesy of San Francisco History Center, San Francisco Public Library.)

Here is a 1904 view of the Hunters Point dry docks and the hills behind them. (Courtesy of a private collector.)

In the late 1800s, the shipyards along Hunters Point used long narrow buildings such as those shown in this image as offices, workshops, and storage containers for lumber and boat parts. Some of the structures were even used as housing. The buildings in the foreground of this photograph are believed to have been used by the Siemers for their boatyard. (Courtesy of the Siemer family.)

Today this building looks much the same as it did when it was built. It is believed to have been built in 1870 by local boat builder William Stone because he was the first person to list this location for his business. Designed in the San Francisco Stick/Eastlake style, it is a one-story-over-basement, wood-frame, single-family workers' cottage. The small size of this building reminds us that India Basin was a working-class neighborhood. (Courtesy of Erin Farrell.)

In 1905, Bethlehem Steel purchased the United States Shipbuilding Corporation, formerly Union Iron, for $1 million. In 1908, the company purchased the Hunters Point dry docks, adding to their own docks on Potrero Hill. Joseph J. Tynan, vice president of Bethlehem Shipbuilding Corporation, is on the far left and his son J. J. "Buster" Tynan Jr. is on the far right. (Courtesy of Lita Jane Tynan Smith.)

Men watch as the first shovelful of earth is turned to make way for the $2 million graving dock of the Union Iron Works Company at Hunters Point. At the time, this was the largest graving dock in the world. (Courtesy of Lita Jane Tynan Smith.)

Workers scramble to get this ship ready for battle. (Courtesy of Lita Jane Smith.)

This is a propeller-machining attachment for a 12-foot Bement boring mill. (Courtesy of Lita Jane Tynan Smith.)

The U.S. destroyer *McKee* launched on March 23, 1918. (Courtesy of Lita Jane Tynan Smith.)

On April 6, 1918, hundreds of people came to the Hunters Point dry docks to celebrate the raising of the flag on Liberty Day. (Courtesy of Lita Jane Tynan Smith.)

This is an aerial view of the shipyards owned and operated by Bethlehem Steel. (Courtesy of Lita Jane Tynan Smith.)

Joseph J. Tynan Sr. built a smaller version of the large ships constructed by Bethlehem Steel so that his son J. J. "Buster" Tynan Jr. could fulfill his boating passions. The photograph was taken September 18, 1918. (Courtesy of Lita Jane Tynan Smith.)

Special launch pictures like this one with Miss Margaret Tynan on January 11, 1919, were popular memorabilia. The U.S. submarine *S32 January* was one of 18 submarines launched from San Francisco. (Courtesy of Lita Jane Tynan Smith.)

Sea Scouts salute prior to a ship's launch into battle. (Courtesy of Lita Jane Tynan Smith.)

The *Challenger* is launched, and the docks with layers of scaffolding and numerous cranes await the next ship. (Courtesy of Lita Jane Tynan Smith.)

During World War I, a new ship was launched practically every day. (Courtesy of Lita Jane Smith.)

Tall sailing ships were also built at the Hunters Point dry docks, and many other shipbuilding companies sat along the waterfront. (Courtesy of Lita Jane Tynan Smith.)

Repairing ships and performing general maintenance was all part of the work done at the dry docks. Seen here are men working to repair the USS *Beaver*. (Courtesy of Lita Jane Tynan Smith.)

COLLISION DAMAGE
"SS BEAVER"

In the late 1920s, many private boats and some local ferries were abandoned at India Basin. In this photograph, the slightly tipping boat is the *Arrow*, which was part of the Monticello Steamship Company's Vallejo route. Also shown, with their paddle wheels and engines removed, are the Southern Pacific Steamers *Apache* and *Modoc*, named for the Indian tribes. (Courtesy of a private collector.)

The USS *New Mexico* is in dry dock at Hunters Point on March 29, 1920. This ship carried President Wilson home from the Versailles Peace Conference, later became a flagship for the new Pacific Fleet, spent 12 years on combined maneuvers with the Atlantic Fleet, was eventually overhauled and modernized, and went on to receive six battle stars for service in World War II. (Courtesy of Lita Jane Tynan Smith.)

The SS *Invincible*, painted with wartime camouflage, sits off Hunters Point. (Courtesy of Lita Jane Tynan Smith.)

Boat builders like Anderson Christofani also constructed boats for the war effort. This photograph was taken in 1942 as part of the launch celebration for this inter-island cargo boat. Fourth and fifth from the left in the second row are John and Flip Allemand. Receiving a pin from a Navy representative is Al Christofani. This is also the boatyard that built Jack London's boat, *The Snark*. (Courtesy of Rene "Flip" Allemand.)

After the launch of each boat, builders, family, and friends would celebrate with a barbeque. This party was for the launch of the boat pictured above. In the front row to the far right with the hat is Harry Anderson; to his left is Rene "Flip" Allemand. (Courtesy of Rene "Flip" Allemand.)

In the late 1930s, Joe Bozel asked John Allemand and his friend Woody to construct him a place to repair boats with an apartment on the second story. It was built next to Joe's Tavern. John and his brother Rene "Flip" Allemand (inside the machinery) helped build boats for the Navy during World War II. In 1962, John and Flip started Allemand Brothers Boatyard. Eventually Joe's Tavern, which had already been moved when the beaches were filled in, became the office space for Allemand Brothers. (Courtesy of Rene "Flip" Allemand.)

The Allemand Brothers Boatyard is seen here in 2005. (Courtesy of author.)

Four

PEOPLE

At age three, Rico Ghilardi was learning to tend to the chickens. The Ghilardis used the chickens for their own consumption as well as for poultry in their store on Williams Avenue. Chicken coops, rabbit hutches, goats, and other animals were common fixtures in Bayview backyards. (Courtesy of Rico Ghilardi.)

Engel met Alvina Bruin, who was indentured as a maid, on a ship sailing to America. They built this house on Revere Street in the 1880s and added to it the 1930s. In 1906, Alvina, Frances, Albert, Moxi, Dot, Martha, and the stable boy posed for this family photograph. (Courtesy of Norma Kruse.)

This house is the oldest still standing in Bayview. Built on Oakdale Avenue in the 1850s, the architectural style is known as "Carpenter's Gothic" or "Steamboat Gothic." It was first owned by John Hittell, who, with his brother Theodore, founded the Academy of Sciences. From 1868 to 1900, the Godeus family lived here, and then they started renting it out. In 1926, the Gouygou family purchased the house. They installed a basement and the first electricity in the house. Gouygou worked at Legallet Tannery. His family stayed there until 1950; another family lived there until 1975. It has been sold several times since then and is now being restored after narrowly escaping demolition. (Courtesy of Mary Grasso Kreutzer.)

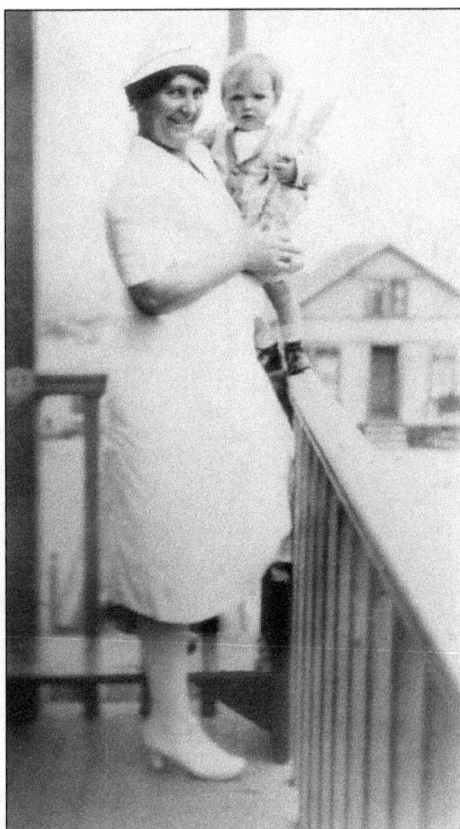

Standing on the porch is little Theresa with her Auntie Katherine Maranto. In the background is the Inn on Innes, owned by Theresa's grandparents, Josephine and William Schabert. (Courtesy of Mary Lou Lawless Mauer.)

Most people had cows or some sort of livestock in their yards. Here Dick Lawless is distracted by the camera as he watches over his cows in the early 1930s. (Courtesy of Mary Lou Lawless Mauer.)

This example of Italianate architecture was built on McKinnon Street around 1870 and owned by Mary Quinn. The house has two stories with a wooden frame, a slanted bay window, a projecting porch entrance in the front, and it sits directly on the ground with no basement. The family owned the house for 83 years. In the 1950s, two Quinn sisters lived there, one upstairs and one downstairs. Unfortunately, they didn't get along and one day the downstairs sister painted the house, stopping just below the second-story windows. It is now a city landmark and being restored by its present owner. (Courtesy of author.)

Eileen Ross Washington became the first African American homeowner in the Bayview Hunters Point district when she purchased her home at 1371 Palou Avenue. A dynamic lady, she made her way to San Francisco from Tahoe, Texas, in the 1930s, looking for a better life. Eileen was also a very religious woman and took great pride in helping to found the Bells Chapel at 1397 Palou Avenue. (Courtesy of Oscar James.)

Mrs. Schabert kept a spotless kitchen. This kitchen was considered fancy in its day, with white walls and red trim. (Courtesy of Mary Lou Lawless Mauer.)

This Italianate Victorian known as the Sylvester House is now a city landmark. The farmhouse was designed and built in 1865 by Steven Piper for Daniel and Maria Sylvester and their eight children. It was originally on Sumatra Street, which in 1911 became Quesada Avenue. At that time, the house was sold to the Faggiones for about $100 on the condition it be moved so the Sylvesters could build something more modern. The house now sits on Revere Street and is being restored to its original splendor. (Courtesy of Mary Grasso Kreutzer.)

In 1934, Michael Lawless tends to his garden on Innes Avenue. (Courtesy of Mary Lou Lawless Mauer.)

Mr. and Mrs. Lawless, along with their children Dick, Terri, Bill, and Mary, lived on Innes Avenue between Mendell and Lane Streets when it was terraced and the family had to walk upstairs to get to the house. Now the street is split-level and raised. (Courtesy of Mary Lou Lawless Mauer.)

During the 1930s, Mary and Louis Meyer and Mrs. Lawless enjoy the backyard with an empty Hunters Point Hill behind them. (Courtesy of Mary Lou Lawless Mauer.)

Mr. Schabert was a well-known builder in the area. In this lot on Innes Avenue, next to his boarding house, he had already built two homes and moved them. Schabert holds a sign that reads, "For sale by owner, 2 lots for $2500 each, inquire at 1456 Innes Avenue." (Courtesy of Mary Lou Lawless Mauer.)

Now here's some initiative. Bill Dunn has figured out a new way to put the livestock to work to suit his needs. This was taken in front of his house on Newcomb Avenue. (Courtesy of Rita Dunn.)

Joyce Turner and her friend Diane play in the front yard of the house on Galvez Street, first owned by her relative Elizabeth O'Brien. (Courtesy of Joyce and Robert Turner.)

Everyone knew the infamous and discreet Mary "Dago Mary" Ghiozo, seen in this photograph with her husband George and their dog in front of a fireplace that came around Cape Horn in the 1890s for James Flood's home in Atherton. Mary ran a popular establishment for eating and entertainment. The restaurant opened in the early 1930s under the name the Venetian Villa, and later became known as Dago Mary's. A seven-course meal with a floor show cost $1.25, and the taxi ride home was $1.35 with tip. A majority of her customers were city politicians. In the mid-1950s, the Navy took it over as their Chief Petty Officers Club. In 1980, it reopened under private owners and remains open to the public today in its original location next to the gates of the Hunters Point shipyard. (Courtesy of Joe and Giacomo James Ursino.)

In the 1920s, hiking out to the water to swim was a popular adventure for children like Art and Johnny McGrath. It was lucky they didn't get sick because just around the bend the sewer pipes spilled into the bay. The kids didn't care. It was too much fun to go out to Shag Rock, the Bluff, or to Bareass Cove—which was for boys only. (Courtesy of Raymond "Jiggy" McGrath.)

During the 1920s, the Verings owned this house on McKinnon Street at Newhall Street. Their daughter Antoinette graduated from Joan of Arc School in 1932. The Verings worked across the street in their French bakery. (Courtesy of author.)

Tal McGrath eats a sandwich after a hike on the hill. (Courtesy of Raymond "Jiggy" McGrath.)

Mary and Louis Meyer were married on February 22, 1934, at All Hallows Church. The couple met in 1926. (Courtesy of Mary Lou Lawless Mauer.)

Mr. McGrath stands in front of his house on Palou Avenue. He had eight children living in a one-bedroom house. Eventually another room was added in the back for the children. However, it was crowded and if one had to get up in the middle of the night he was usually punched on his way out. (Courtesy of Raymond "Jiggy" McGrath.)

Anthony McGrath is dressed up for his first communion day. Most days he could be found climbing to the roof of the Smith house next door and running the neighborhood with his buddies. Benny Lamb is in the background. This block of Palou Avenue was home to the Fox, Lamb, and Wolf families. Coincidentally the Lambs and Foxes were related. (Courtesy of Raymond "Jiggy" McGrath.)

At this house on Newcomb Avenue there is a sign in the window with stars on it—one star for each person serving in the armed forces. Anyone who had a family member in the service displayed this sign. This family had three members overseas, two in the Army and one in the Navy. Grandma Dunn sat under this window every day and waited for the postman to arrive. Pictured here, from left to right, are (first row) Gert Dunn Fern, Raymond "Lovey" Dunn, Evelyn Dunn DiGiacoma, and Peg "Grandma" Dunn; (second row) Frances "Hon" Dunn Pereira holding her son Larry, Pat Fern, and Sandy Fern. (Courtesy of Rita Dunn.)

The Oosterman's house on Palou Avenue shows a typical Bayview neighborhood backyard. (Courtesy of Rita Oosterman.)

Here is a picture of the Navy's girls volleyball team champions. (Courtesy of Raymond "Jiggy" McGrath.)

This cast of characters that made up the Stampede Citizens Committee of Leaders to help celebrate the World's Fair are John J. Ryan, general chairman; Dr. L. R. Ludwigsen, parade; Tony Devencenzi, decorations; A. Armanino, finance; Cecelia Milly, secretary; Herb Elvander, entertainment; and Joe Flores, publicity. (Courtesy of Dr. Larry Ludwigsen.)

This new police station was built, but never used as an official police station. Instead it was used as a place for the kids to hang out and stay out of trouble. (Courtesy of Mary Grasso Kreutzer.)

The St. Joan of Arc Church altar boys pose for a picture after mass. (Courtesy of Rita Oosterman.)

Giovanni Baumgartner built this house at 1297 Palou Avenue for his family in 1913. Posing in this 1917 photograph, from left to right, are George Joseph Baumgartner, Barbara Maria (Turco) Baumgartner, Giovanni Baumgartner, and an unknown woman. Sitting in a chair, holding a cat, is Alice Baumgartner, and sitting on the step is George's twin sister Lilly Anne Baumgartner. The family was originally from Castelnuovo d'Asti, Italy. Giovanni owned North Beach Jewelers on Stockton Street and he also sold jewelry out of the front room on the left side of his house. Lilly eventually had the porch enclosed so she could raise and sell canaries. In 1926, Lilly Baumgartner married James Diamond in this house. (Courtesy of the Lilly Baumgartner Diamond family.)

On September 25, 1949, Rico and June kiss next to their 1948 Packard. They went to Latona Street to the home of good friend Walter Mazzei, of Mazzei Hardware, to take photographs after the wedding. (Courtesy of Rico Ghilardi.)

The neighborhood may not have been the fancy part of town, but fashion was still part of a lady's life. Women never left the house without their hat and gloves. Here Eleanor Sheehan shows off her new hat. (Courtesy of the Eleanor Sheehan family.)

May is traditionally known as the month of the "Blessed Mother Mary." To celebrate, the school would have the entire student body make a human rosary, and there was also a procession and crowning of Mary. Shown here, from left to right, are Mary Lou Lawless, Peggy Andrade, and Nancy Ferraris, who were selected to play special roles in the May crowning event. Peggy was selected to place the crown on Mary. (Courtesy of Mary Lou Lawless Mauer.)

Fifteen-year-old Rico Ghilardi delivers groceries for his father in this 1938 photograph. (Courtesy of Rico Ghilardi.)

The Bayview Grocery Store stood on Williams Avenue and Ceres Street. (Courtesy of Rico Ghilardi.)

Mr. and Mrs. Ghilardi pose inside their store, the Bayview Grocery. (Courtesy of Rico Ghilardi.)

The movie theatre used to advertise in the window of the Bayview Grocery. In exchange, Mrs. Ghilardi got movie tickets. (Courtesy of Rico Ghilardi.)

Kids played outside and ran around the neighborhood. Everyone knew and watched out for one another. (Courtesy of Rico Ghilardi.)

Kids play in the extra space of the now widened Williams Avenue. (Courtesy of Rico Ghilardi.)

On a Sunday afternoon in 1943, John and Joe McGrath, Moon Cotter, and Tal McGrath hang out in their backyard on Palou Avenue. (Courtesy of Raymond "Jiggy" McGrath.)

Seen here in a new jeep in 1945 are Rico Ghilardi and Guido Ghiselli, ready to go into the gas station business. Rico opened a grocery store instead, then years later went into the car business. (Courtesy of Rico Ghilardi.)

Alice Petrale Trapani was involved in everything. She grew up in a house on Revere Street near the bay. The Trapanis had a dozen cows and would sell the milk in the neighborhood. In 1932, she went into real estate, and asked Yvonne Picard to work with her. Their first listing, which sold for $28,000, was Juliette Denike's house. (Courtesy of All Hallows Church.)

Bayview was known as the salad bowl of the city. Mr. and Mrs. Armanino had the last truck garden on Williams Avenue. Kraft Foods bought chives from them to use in their cheese. What started as a small neighborhood garden eventually grew into a large company that is still in business today. (Courtesy of Dr. Larry Ludwigsen.)

During the Stampede Costume Ball to celebrate the 1939 World's Fair, Frank "Lefty" O'Doul received an invitation to dance from Irene Lepphaille. Lefty O'Doul was born on Galvez Avenue to a French mother and Irish father. He attended Bayview Elementary School. (Courtesy of Dr. Larry Ludwigsen.)

"Lefty" O'Doul's principal, Mrs. Stokes, saw something in him and encouraged him to swing that bat and play ball as much as possible. Whenever Stokes felt Lefty was in a slump and needed a boost, she would line up the children in the school yard and make them yell a cheer so Lefty could hear—"When you're up you're up, when you're down you're down, when you're up against Lefty you're upside down!" (Courtesy of the San Francisco History Center, San Francisco Public Library.)

In 1946, the All Hallows crossing guards are standing in formation as part of Traffic Boys Day. All public, private, and parochial schools with crossing guards participated in this event. (Courtesy of Rita Oosterman.)

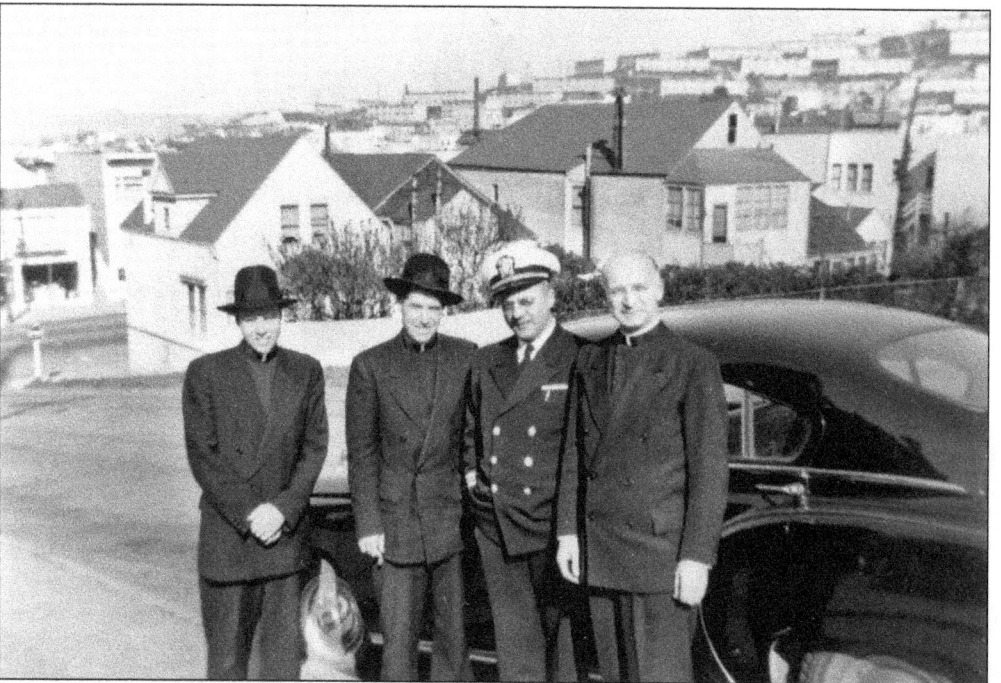

In 1950, standing outside of All Hallows Church on Newhall Street between Palou and Oakdale Avenues are Father Duke, Father Collins, navy chaplain Father Ouelette, and Father Chouinard. (Courtesy of Fr. Patrick Coyle.)

Here is the Magnaghi family on Oakdale Avenue outside of St. Paul the Shipwreck Church. They owned the Swiss Italian Sausage Company at 4401 Third Street. Note that the new Burnett School stands behind them. (Courtesy of Rita Dunn.)

It was customary to walk to the beach for a family outing. This location at Gilman Park in Candlestick Cove provided a barbecue area for family picnics. At the end of the pier was a snack shack that sold bait for fishing, sandwiches, drinks, and treats. Eventually this beach was filled in to make way for the parking lot at Candlestick Park. Standing in front of one of the barbecues are Pete, Cristina, John, and Vera Sutti in 1941. (Courtesy of Edie Sutti Epps collection.)

Butchertown came out in force to support Mayor Elmer Robinson's efforts for reelection. A rally was held outside of the Four-Mile House, a popular restaurant in Butchertown. Windmills, like the one under the banner on the left, were once common on the hillside. (Courtesy of Dr. Larry Ludwigsen.)

On the podium for the reelection rally are Mayor Robinson, Mr. Filippi, and L. R. Ludwigsen. (Courtesy of Dr. Larry Ludwigsen.)

Tony Devencenzi, owner of the Four-Mile House, and Fred Dettmering barbeque lunch for the neighborhood supporters of Mayor Robinson. (Courtesy of Dr. Larry Ludwigsen.)

Sam Jordan was known as the mayor of Butchertown. In 1947, Sam arrived in San Francisco, and quickly became a regular in the boxing scene under the name "Singing Sam" because he sang the national anthem and other songs before and after his fights. In 1948, he won the diamond belt in the light heavyweight championships of the San Francisco Golden Gloves Tournament. In 1959, he opened a bar and restaurant on Third Street called Sam Jordan's. It was the place to go for entertainment, and many celebrities would stop by—including Sammy Davis Jr. In 1963, he was the first African American to run for mayor of San Francisco. Although he came in fourth (Jack Shelley won the election), Sam was truly committed to improving his community. Over the years, he employed as many as 400 neighborhood residents and offered help to hundreds more. (Courtesy of Sam and Ruth Jordan.)

Five

CHURCHES AND SCHOOLS

The people are what made the neighborhood so unique. This 1918 class photograph represents typical children in the neighborhood pre–World War I. (Courtesy of Rico Ghilardi.)

In the early 1900s, neighbors and school officials celebrate the laying of the cornerstone for the Bayview School on Bayview and Flora Avenues. (Courtesy of Dr. Larry Ludwigsen.)

Many of the children in Miss E. Walsh's first-grade class from the Bayview Elementary School were second or third generation students. Seen here in December 1947, from left to right, are (first row) Juliette, Anna, Carlos, Sammy, Lolita Escalante, Gordon Morrio, and Frank Duran; (second row) Diane Douglas, Joseph Singlaterry, Bobbie Martin, Dickie Lewellyn, George Babbas, Gerald Manini, and Billie Casella; (third row) Joyce Turner, Tommy, Shirley McAteer, Dorothy Foster, Deanna Papera, Amos, and Mary Lee Fannuchi. (Courtesy of Joyce and Robert Turner.)

Many children in Bayview Hunters Point attended the Bret Harte public school shown here on Third Street and Le Conte Avenue. The school was later purchased for $1 from the city by St. Paul the Shipwreck Church. Bret Harte School then moved to Gilman Avenue. (Courtesy of Jack Tillmany.)

This building was once the St. Joan of Arc School and stands where All Hallows School used to be at Quesada Avenue and Lane Street. Originally half of the building was a school, where students entered through the door on the left, and the other half was used as a convent to house the nuns. In 1952, it was renovated and became the Sisters of St. Joseph's convent. In June 1991, Catholic Charities purchased the building and opened Jelani House, Incorporated, to assist the community with issues such as substance abuse and infant survival. (Courtesy of Fr. Patrick Coyle.)

Program

Dedication of the Burnett School

Sunday, August 27th, 1911

☙

Parade of Improvement Club and other organizations from Fifth and Railroad Ave. to School House.

F. W. Zimmerman, Grand Marshal

Presentation of Silver Trowel to His Honor, P. H. McCarthy, Mayor of San Francisco
Laying of Corner Stone

Dedication

1. **Overture** . . . . Band
2. **Children's Chorus** . . . ."Our Flag"
3. **Flag Raising** . . . . Professor Geo. S. Miehling
4. **Flag Salute** . . . . Pupils of Burnett School
    Under direction of Miss L. McElroy, Principal.
5. **Introductory Remarks** . . . .
    Pres. T. L. Sharman introducing Supervisor C. A. Nelson, Pres. of the Day
6. **Children's Chorus** . . . .(a) "Spring Song" Rubenstein; (b) "Old
    Black Joe"; (c) "Columbia the Gem of the Ocean"
7. **Address** . . . . By Supt. of Schools A. Roncovieri
8. **Children's Chorus** . . . . Intermezzo from Cavalleri Rusticana
9. **Address** . . . . Hon. P. H. McCarthy, Mayor of San Francisco
10. **Children's Chorus** . . . .(a) My Country" Stewart (b) Anvil Chorus"
    Il Trovatore, Verdi
11. **Music** . . . . .By Band
12. **Address** . . . . By Phillip Prior, of the Bay View Grammar School
13. **Children's Chorus** . . . .(a) "My Fatherland"; (b) "Funiculi,
    Funicula," Denza; (c) "Star Spangeled Banner"

Music under the direction of Miss E. Carpenter, Supervisor

BUCKLEY ☙ CURTIN

Pictured here is the 1911 dedication program for Burnett School. (Courtesy of Dr. Larry Ludwigsen.)

This building is the original Burnett School built in 1911. The school was eventually moved to Oakdale Avenue. Notice Mount St. Joseph in the background. (Courtesy of Dr. Larry Ludwigsen.)

Here is a 1931 class photograph from Burnett School. (Courtesy of Raymond "Jiggy" McGrath.)

St. Joan of Arc Church on La Salle Avenue was built in 1922 to take care of the needs of the French people in the neighborhood. It was served by the Marist fathers of Our Lady of Victory Church, mother church of the French colony of San Francisco. (Courtesy of Rita Oosterman.)

This 1946 photograph show the Sisters of St. Joseph of Orange who ran the school at St. Joan of Arc. The Sisters devote their lives to teaching nursing and missionary work. (Courtesy of Rita Oosterman.)

This is a photograph of the drama club at St. Joan of Arc Church. (Courtesy of Rita Oosterman.)

Benny and Bobby Oosterman are ready for school in their St. Joan of Arc uniforms in 1938. (Courtesy of Rita Oosterman.)

St. Paul the Shipwreck Church is known as the Maltese church. In 1915, Reverend Azzopardi purchased a hall that had been built in 1874 on Oakdale Avenue, and gave it to the Maltese to use as their church. Reverend Azzopardi retired in 1919 and Rev. Theophilus Cachia took over. He was a favorite with the children, and was well-known for his after-school snacks, activities, and hikes on Hunters Point. (Courtesy of Mary Grasso Kreutzer.)

Early 1950s students of St. Paul the Shipwreck school pose for a traditional first communion photograph (with the boys on one side and girls on the other side). Rev. Benvenute Bavero, more commonly referred to as "Father Benny," is in the back row. Father Benny was very popular in the community and well remembered by the students for his after-school snacks and outdoor activities. St. Paul the Shipwreck was named after the patron saint of Malta. Legend has it that by an act of the apostles, Paul was shipwrecked on the island of Malta. (Courtesy Cathy Kline.)

90

The 1961 Flahavan wedding ceremony took place inside St. Paul the Shipwreck Church. (Courtesy of Lillian Flahavan.)

All Hallows Church was built in 1886 on the corner of Palou Avenue and Newhall Street. The first parishioners of what is now All Hallows parish began to congregate in 1852 in the chapel of the Catholic Orphan Asylum. In 1868, Fr. Timothy Fitzpatrick, the first pastor at All Hallows, became chaplain of the orphanage. He created the parish and built the church, naming it after the seminary he had attended in Dublin, Ireland. (Courtesy of a private collector.)

In this 1950s image, the workforce of the All Hallows parish includes, from left to right, unidentified, Mrs. Marchessi, four unidentified women, Mrs. Lyons (top with glasses), Lydabelle Robinson, Nellie Pressans, (lower) Mrs. Oosterman, Mrs. Reno, Irene Molinari, Della Wehram, and Mrs. Martin. (Courtesy of Rita Oosterman.)

Here is the inside of All Hallows Church during mass. (Courtesy of All Hallows Church.)

ALL HALLOWS MAY FESTIVAL

A Benefit For The New School and Convent

—— AT ——

YOUTH CENTER BUILDING

QUESADA AVENUE and LANE STREET
(One Block Off Third Street)

FRIDAY, SATURDAY & SUNDAY

MAY 26th, 27th and 28th

MRS. IGNATIUS TRAPANI & MR. ROBERT McCARTHY
Co-Chairmen

ADMISSION FREE   EVERYONE WELCOME

★

Dessert-Fashion Show and Musicale

Saturday, May 27th, 1 p.m., New Auditorium

REVERE AVENUE and LANE STREET—$1.00

Reservations can be made with Mrs. Ignatius Trapani
1570 REVERE AVENUE - MI 7-6586

This flyer is for a 1948 fund-raising event for the new All Hallows School. (Courtesy of All Hallows Church.)

On Sunday, April 3, 1949, Father Collins officiates the groundbreaking ceremony for All Hallows new parochial school. (Courtesy of All Hallows Church.)

Sylvester House is in the background of this photograph of the dedication ceremony of All Hallows School. (Courtesy of All Hallows Church.)

Sr. Hortense Marie stands with her students in her new kindergarten classroom at All Hallows School in 1949. (Courtesy of All Hallows Church.)

Sr. M. Eugenie poses with her students in her new eighth-grade classroom at All Hallows School in the fall of 1949. (Courtesy of All Hallows Church.)

Here are the proud graduates of All Hallows School class of 1966. (Courtesy of All Hallows Church.)

Kids play in the yard during recess at All Hallows School in the 1970s. (Courtesy of All Hallows Church.)

These two images show Our Lady of Lourdes Church, dedicated January 25, 1942. The intention of the style was to embody the traditional California mission look. With the increasing number of workers at the shipyard, it became a convenient location to worship. Mrs. Andrew Welch led the effort to build the church and collect donations for the altar, organ, and other features inside the building. (Courtesy of author.)

Inside of the church is the statue of *Our Lady of Providence*. To the left is the art window of Jesus blessing the little children. (Courtesy of author.)

Opening in 1871, this is one of the oldest churches in the neighborhood. It was originally known as the South San Francisco Methodist-Episcopal Church. Still located on the corner of Bayview and Latona Streets, it is now known as the Pearlgate Tabernacle Baptist Church, founded by Rev. Isaac H. Flippin on September 21, 1969. (Courtesy of author.)

Six

THIRD STREET

This June 17, 1944, photograph
is Third Street at Revere
Street looking north toward
Quesada Avenue. Petersen's
furniture store is on the corner,
then the Bayview Theatre
and Stella's Floral Shop.
(Courtesy of Jack Tillmany.)

Solari Flats ran along Third Street between Kirkwood and La Salle Avenues. The bottom floor held businesses such as the Butcher's Union, Solari's market, the Bayview Fish Market, a bar, the French laundry, and a poultry shop. The top portion contained flats for the owners and their renters. (Courtesy of Rita Dunn.)

Joseph Solari owned a liquor store just up the street from his other property, Solari Flats, where he lived. He had two business partners, brothers Angelo and John Righetti. (Courtesy of Rita Dunn.)

The Bayview Fish Market was just one of the shops in the row called Solari Flats on Third Street between Kirkwood and La Salle Avenues. Rita Solari stopped in one day and was asked to model for the owners as they photographed their catch of the day. (Courtesy of Rita Dunn.)

Since it opened in 1937, Mazzei Hardware has been at the same location on Third Street. Gene Mazzei opened the store and it has continued to be family owned ever since. This photograph was taken in 1939. The building is still the same, only the equipment sold has been updated. (Courtesy of the Mazzei family.)

The Bayview Theatre was on Third Street between Palou and Quesada Avenues, and was owned by Otto Rodder. Before sound, viewers could watch two cowboy and Indian shows, a chapter in a serial, and a comedy. The day sound came to the theatre, Mr. Otto had comedian Ben Turpin from Hollywood perform in front of the theatre. "Mr. Otto" and his young bride from Germany owned a house on Lane Street and Palou Avenue which was known as quite the fashionable place. Paul Gatt eventually took ownership of the theatre. (Courtesy of Jack Tillmany.)

The Bayview Theatre once held a raffle for a tea set. No one ever won, but Stanley Pudlow did come running down the aisle one day saying he had the winning number. He didn't, but Mr. Otto Rodder nearly had a heart attack. (Courtesy of Jack Tillmany.)

Bay View Federal Savings opened on November 18, 1911, in a tiny office next to a barbershop on Railroad Avenue. Because Bayview residents were being left out of the downtown financial world, a group in the neighborhood decided to form their own company to provide residents with a place to keep their savings or to obtain a home loan. Each contributed $700 as capital and drew up a charter establishing Bay View Building and Loan Association as a mutual institution. On August 5, 1919, the office moved to Third Street and Oakdale Avenue and paid $35 a month in rent. (Courtesy Rita Oosterman.)

The streetcar passing A. J. Parodi's Garage was often a victim of children's sling shots. Mr. Parodi chose gravel instead of tar—much to the delight of the young boys. The only defense the streetcar possessed was the fender or "cow catcher" attached to the front of the car to deflect animals, people, and anything else in its way. (Courtesy of Jack Tillmany.)

Walter J. Peck's Hardware Store on Third Street had ladder rails inside. Whenever someone made a request for items on a high shelf, the ladder would slide back and forth across the store while the store clerk collected the items. Next door was former officer O'Leary's Liquors. (Courtesy of Mary Grasso Kreutzer.)

Hyster sold lift trucks to many of the businesses in the neighborhood. They were located at Third Street and La Salle Avenue. When the building was built in 1949, it was the newest building in the area. (Courtesy of Lillian Flahavan.)

The 4900 block of Third Street was home to the Ronan Meat Market, the Mens and Boys Clothing Store, and George Jones Insurance. Across the street (not shown in this view) was the Bayview Bakery, now the Bayview Barber College, and the ever popular Dutch Mill Creamery where everyone went for a treat. (Courtesy of Betty Jones.)

Everyone knew Arthur Viagras, who owned the Elkhorn Garage on Third Street. He used to brag that his teacher at Burnett School said he was so stupid that he'd be lucky to dig ditches to fix Third Street. She was wrong. He was probably one of the richest guys in the neighborhood. He made quite a bit of money with his tow trucks.

Grasso Properties was located at 5129 Third Street. Natale Grasso came over from Sicily and spoke no English. To break the hard ground so he could build the place, Mr. Grasso poured oil on the ground, set fire to it, then hammered it to level the ground. He first built a house with a store, then another house. (Courtesy of Mary Grasso Kreutzer.)

Here is a streetcar coming off the Third Street Bridge at Islais Creek as it enters the Bayview Hunters Point district. (Courtesy of Jack Tillmany.)

Modesto and Harry Esposto ran Esposto Market at 5030 Third Street near Quesada Avenue. It was the largest market around with a butcher shop and a produce section plus some dry goods. It carried just about everything families needed, and they also delivered. (Courtesy of author.)

In 1940, car 993 on the No. 16 line heads north on Third Street at Paul Avenue. Bombo's Boccie Ball is in the right hand corner. Oggie Ramos was a bartender at Bombos. (Courtesy of Jack Tillmany.)

In 1940, car 958 on the No. 16 line heads southbound on Third Street approaching San Bruno Avenue. Before the freeway was built (1949–1952), Third Street intersected San Bruno Avenue at Wilde Avenue. The Five-Mile House can be seen in the background to the left of the car. (Courtesy of Jack Tillmany.)

Seven

CURRENT DAY

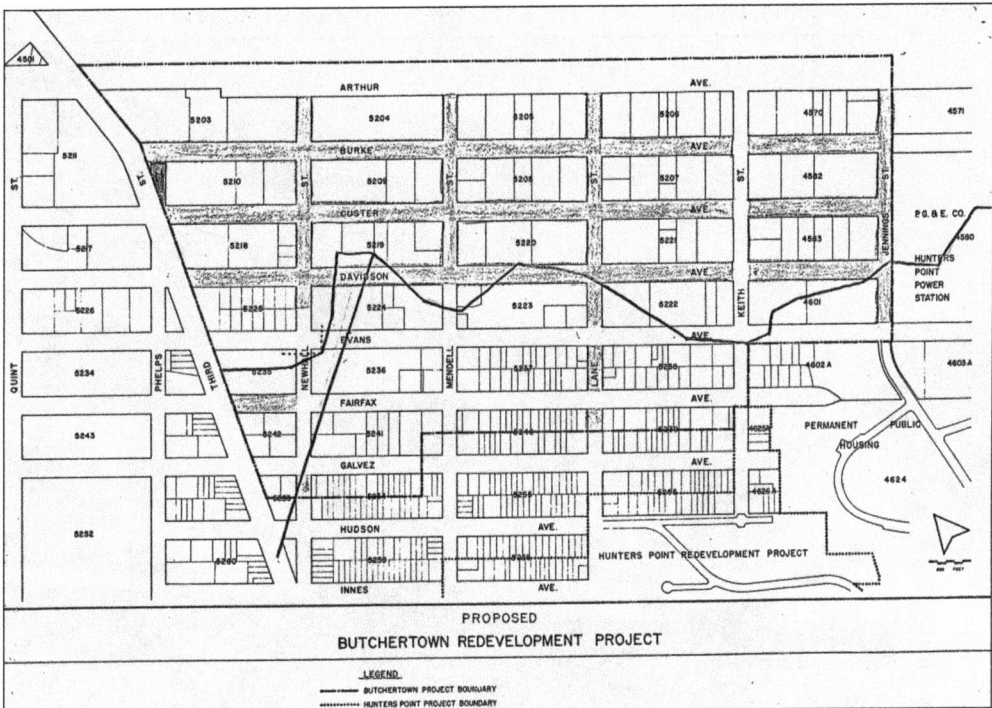

This is a map of the proposed Butchertown Redevelopment Project in the late 1970s. The India Basin Industrial Park inhabits most of this area today. (Courtesy of the San Francisco Redevelopment Agency.)

In 1981, a groundbreaking ceremony for a new complex named All Hallows Community at Newhall Street and Oakdale Avenue, adjacent to All Hallows Church, was held. It was sponsored by Catholic Charities/Catholic Social Services of San Francisco. Participating in the ceremony are Archbishop Quinn, Diane Feinstein, and Art Agnos. (Courtesy of All Hallows Church.)

Here is the residential complex for the elderly and disabled as it looks today. There are 45 apartments, and recreational and social facilities to help the residents maintain their independence (Courtesy of author.)

All Hallows Church still stands in its original location; however the dirt road from the turn of the late 1800s no longer remains. Today Palou Avenue looking west toward Newhall Street is a paved road with rows of houses. (Courtesy of Mary Grasso Kreutzer.)

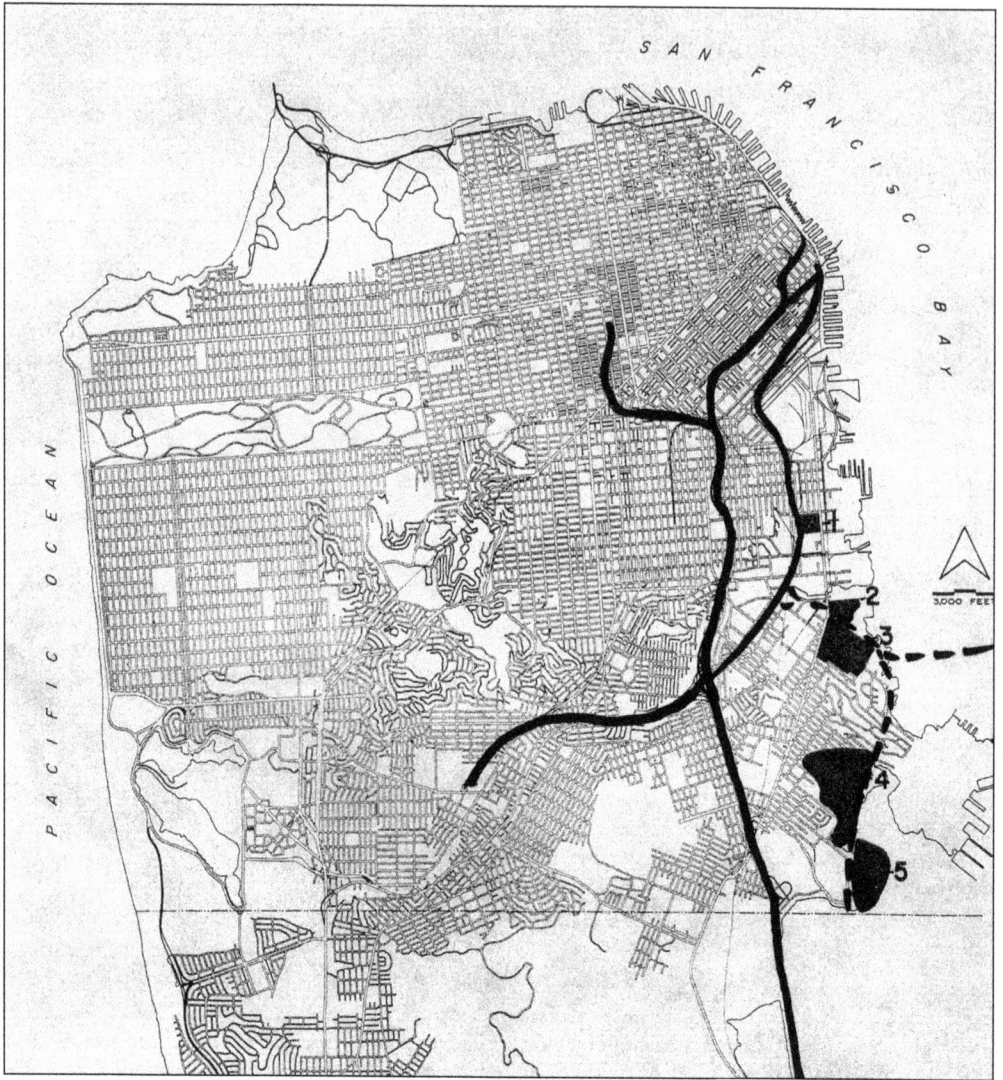

This photograph shows existing and proposed future freeways to accommodate growth in the Bayview Hunters Point district. The five numbered blocks were areas considered for industrial parks. Block number three by India Basin was chosen as the best spot. The dotted lines indicate freeways that were proposed but not built, including a second bay bridge known informally as the "Southern Crossing." (Courtesy of the San Francisco Redevelopment Agency.)

The Third Street Light Rail Project is intended to revitalize the neighborhood by making it easier to travel to and from downtown and Bayview. The rail is five and half miles long with a price tag of $569 million. It is scheduled to open at the end of 2005. (Courtesy of author.)

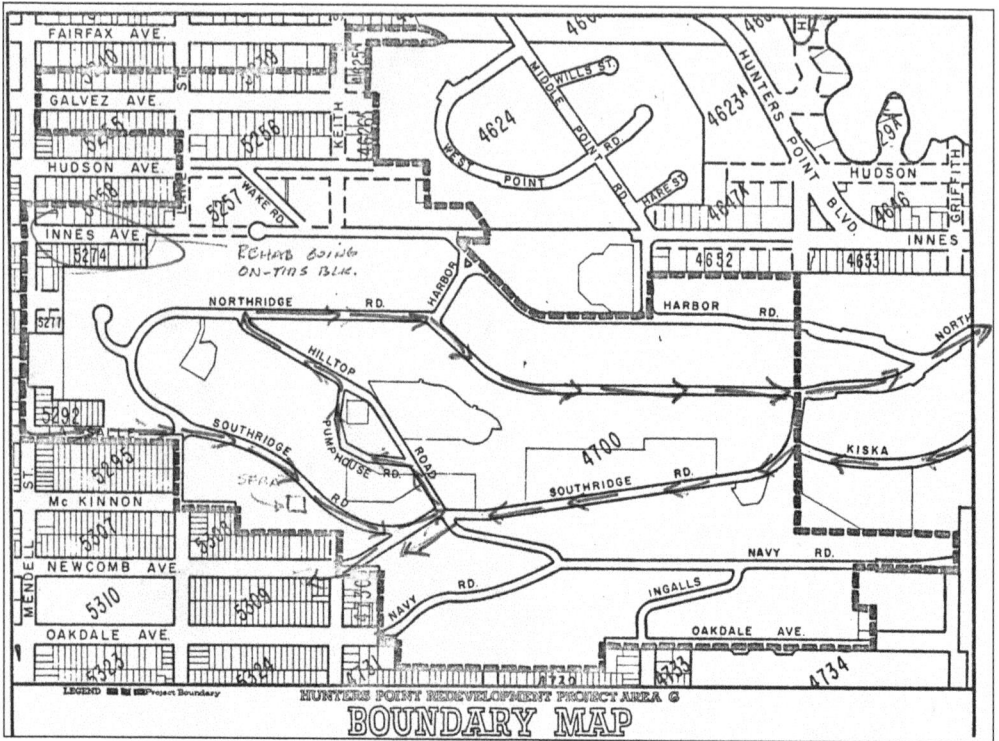

Hunters Point Redevelopment Project Area G

BOUNDARY MAP

This map is the Hunters Point Redevelopment Project Area G boundary map. It shows what the redevelopment agency was considering in August 1970. Note there was already some work started on Innes Avenue and Lane Street. (Courtesy of the San Francisco Redevelopment Agency.)

The Bayview Hunters Point Foundation for Community Improvement is a nonprofit organization founded in 1971 by the citizens of the Bayview Hunters Point, led by the late Ernest Mitchell Jr., to inform, educate, and provide comprehensive multipurpose social and human services. The foundation was created to address the needs of the predominantly African American population with legal assistance, drug and alcohol rehabilitation, and mental health care. Since its inception, the foundation has expanded substantially and now includes programs such as HIV/AIDS support services, extensive mental health services, school-based health services, and health care for the homeless. (Courtesy of author.)

In the 1970s, Mount St. Joseph's Orphanage was torn down to make way for a new housing development at the top of Silver Terrace. (Courtesy of Mary Grasso Kreutzer.)

This house at 146 Innes Avenue is an example of the expandable houses being built in the area as part of the redevelopment effort to enhance housing conditions in the neighborhood. (Courtesy of the San Francisco Redevelopment Agency.)

Opened in 1959, Sam Jordan's is still open for business on Third Street. Although Sam is no longer alive, his family keeps the place going and still serves great barbeque. (Courtesy of author.)

In 2004, Sally Ross opened SYR Gifts at 4923 Third Street, which sells flowers and gift baskets. Her goal is to give back to the community she grew up in, and to provide a positive business atmosphere. (Courtesy of author.)

Serving the neighborhood since 1937, Mazzei Hardware has stood in the same location where it was first built. The inside still has the same wooden floor it started with; only the inventory has been updated. (Courtesy of author.)

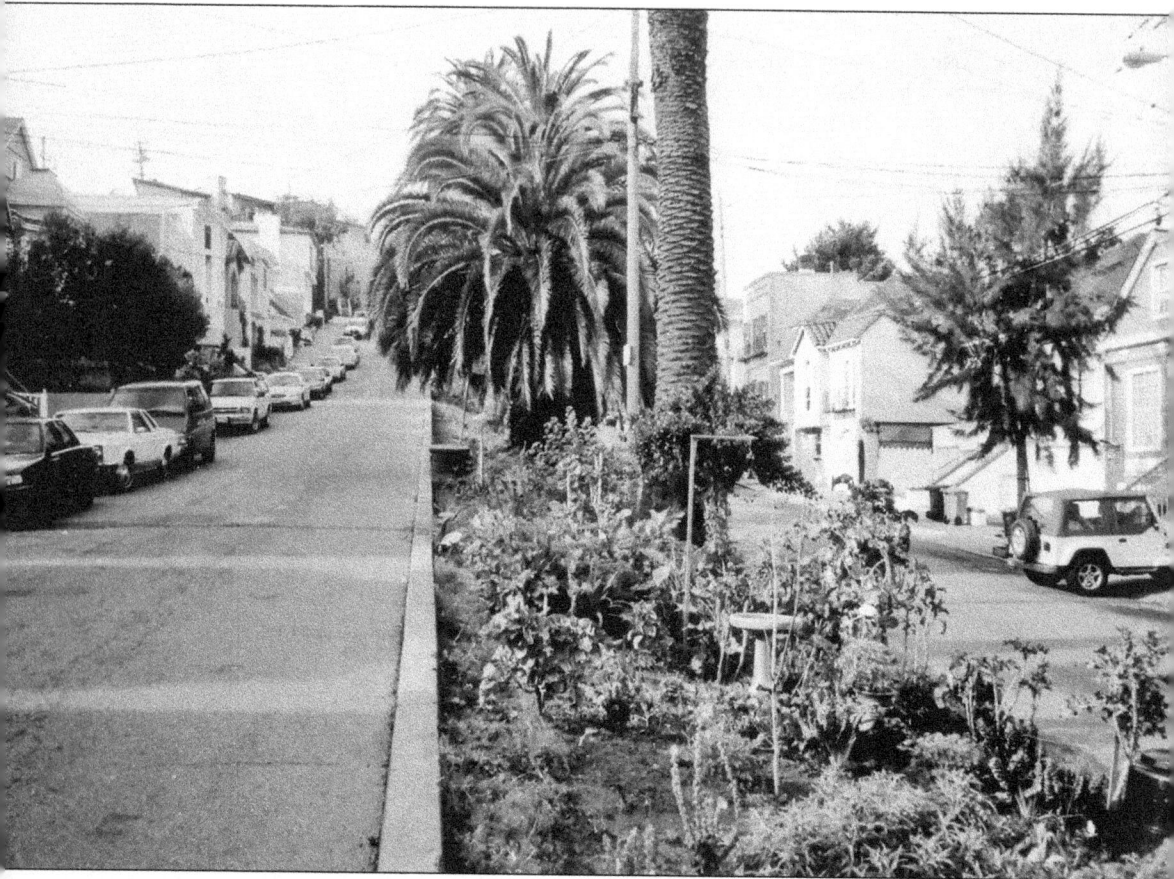

Tired of people hanging out and destroying the street, Annette Young and Karl Paige planted a garden in the median of Quesada Avenue. Neighbors banded together to maintain their efforts. Other streets have started doing the same, not only adding to the beauty of the street, but also increasing safety and positive, friendly neighbor relationships. (Courtesy of author.)

This Federal Revival house on Palou Avenue was once owned by sisters Mabel and Hazel Hofstadter. At one time, there was a carriage house out back and beautiful floral gardens. (Courtesy of Mary Grasso Kreutzer.)

Next door to Mabel and Hazel is the Queen Anne–style house once owned by Mr. McDonald, a blacksmith in the neighborhood. The two houses are quite a unique pairing of architectural styles. (Courtesy of Mary Grasso Kreutzer.)

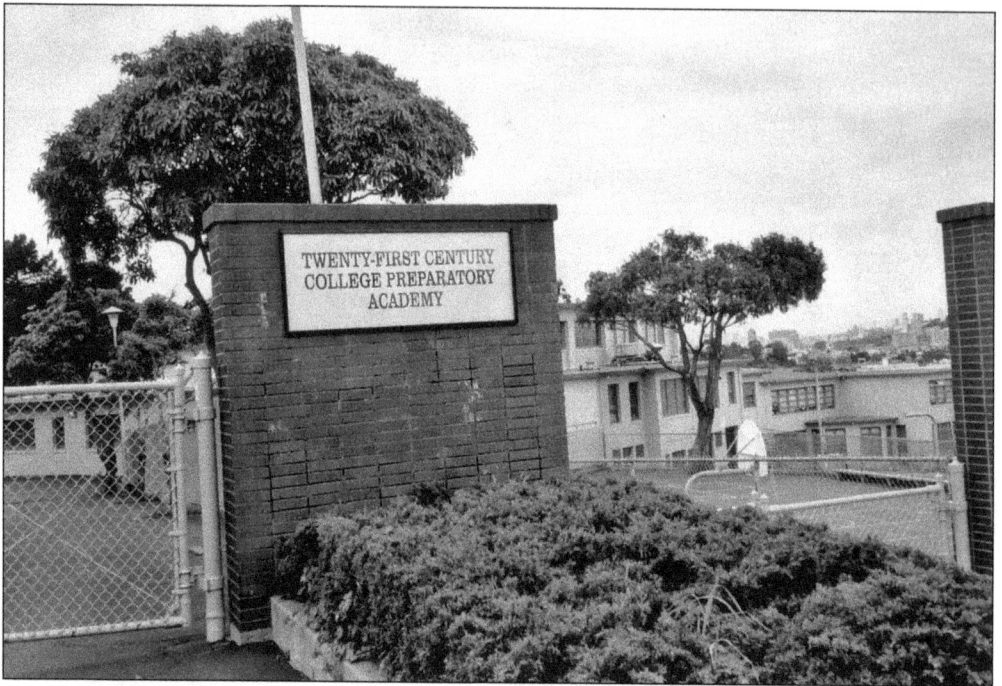

The "Dream Schools" shown here are modeled after the Loraine Monroe model from Harlem. The goal is to take a failing school and install a strict program that students and parents must commit to in order to raise test scores. Opponents claim that the lower performers are not accepted at the school; therefore their needs are still not being met. Three dream schools exist in Bayview Hunters Point. Recently, one of the schools that was slated for closure passed a community vote to stay open. (Courtesy of author.)

The Bayview Anna E. Waden Branch of the San Francisco Public Library system is on the corner of Third and Revere Streets. It is a small branch, but serves as a great resource for the neighborhood. It also has a large archive of neighborhood history. There is a separate area for children to read or participate in the numerous learning programs available each week. (Courtesy of author.)

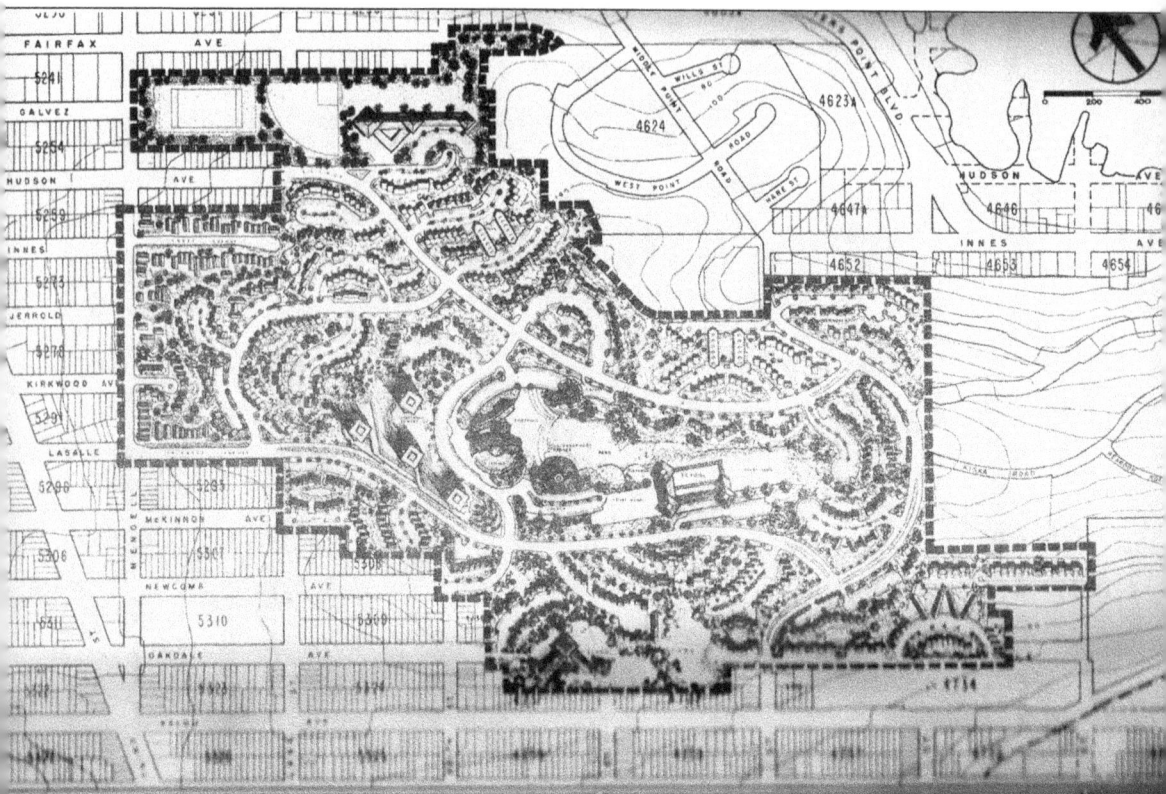

Here is a more detailed map of the San Francisco Redevelopment Agency's proposed Hunters Point housing community in the late 1970s. (Courtesy of the San Francisco Redevelopment Agency.)

The housing projects still standing on Hunters Point were originally built as temporary housing for the shipyard workers during World War II. (Courtesy of the San Francisco Redevelopment Agency.)

The redevelopment agency is trying to create more up-to-date housing. This photograph was taken along Innes Avenue. (Courtesy of the San Francisco Redevelopment Agency.)

An undated aerial view shows the growth that has taken place in this century. (Courtesy of a private collector.)

www.ingramcontent.com/pod-product-compliance
Lightning Source LLC
Chambersburg PA
CBHW050549110426
42813CB00008B/2302